NEW YORK CITY ICONS

New York City

ICONS

50 Classic Slices of the Big Apple

JONATHAN SCHEFF

gpp

Guilford, Connecticut

Photo credits: p. iii apple courtesy Index Open; pp. 24, 44, 53, 54 courtesy Shutterstock; all others by Jonathan Scheff.

Text design by Casey Shain

Library of Congress Cataloging-in-Publication Data

Scheff, Jonathan.
  New York City icons : 50 classic slices of the Big Apple / Jonathan Scheff.
    p. cm.
  ISBN-13: 978-0-7627-4745-0
  1. New York (N.Y.)—Pictorial works. 2. New York (N.Y.)—Social life and customs—Pictorial works. 3. Historic buildings—New York (State)—New York—Pictorial works. 4. Historic sites—New York (State)—New York—Pictorial works. 5. New York (N.Y.)—Buildings, structures, etc.—Pictorial works. 6. New York (N.Y.)—Description and travel. I. Title.
  F128.37.S29 2008
  917.47'10444—dc22

                                                              2008011515

Printed in China

2 4 6 8 10 9 7 5 3 1

"One belongs to New York instantly, one belongs to it as much in five minutes as in five years."
—*Thomas Wolfe*

To New York City, where we all belong.

CONTENTS

INTRODUCTION

Everybody knows New York City. You don't have to live here to have an opinion about it—you don't even have to visit. The city has woven itself so deeply into the fabrics of culture, art, business, fashion, and history that even people in the most remote areas on earth know a thing or two about the Big Apple. It is a meta-icon—or a mega-icon, perhaps—encapsulating all of the figures, structures, and events that have made it famous as well as infamous, including the fifty icons presented here.

Perhaps it is because of New York's international renown that it is a difficult city to characterize, since every person has a different perspective: New York is the most glamorous city in the world, the most romantic, the noisiest, the dirtiest, the best, the worst, the most exciting, the most depressing. No two people have experienced the same New York twice.

Thus there are as many New Yorks as there are people in this world. This book presents just one version, offering fifty of the city's most recognized icons and telling the story of New York's most publicized, most famous, or most controversial accomplishments.

As a journalist and photographer in New York, my adopted home, I have been fortunate to explore some nooks and crannies in all five boroughs. Over my years here, I have interviewed real estate moguls and inmates of the Rikers Island prison; I have found Di Fara pizzeria in Midwood, Brooklyn, where Domenico De Marco makes every single pie, and I have stumbled across hidden treasures like the museum of the Hispanic Society in Washington Heights. But what I've learned more than anything else is that I will never know even one-zillionth of the city's full cultural and historical content.

Consequently I'd like to acknowledge all the New Yorks that don't appear in this book: the few New Yorks with which I am familiar and the infinite New Yorks with which I am not. I especially want to acknowledge all the people who keep the city alive, even if they do not appear in these pages. It is easy to mark New York's history with celebrity: accomplishments like the Brooklyn Bridge and figures like the Roebling family that built it. In the following entries, I have certainly

mentioned several of these figures, including the Rockefellers, Robert Moses, and Rudolph Giuliani. Here, however, I would like to mention the people who run the city day to day, and do it with less recognition: the bus driver who wakes up at three o'clock every morning to drive the M60 bus to LaGuardia Airport; the construction workers who are building the new Yankee Stadium; the librarians at the New York Public Library, whose love for knowledge seeps into the books they govern.

The New York presented in this book is a glorious one indeed. These fifty icons tell many intriguing stories from several centuries of the city's history.

And after you've flipped through these pages, I hope you put down this book and explore the city yourself. The best New York you'll ever experience is your own New York.

NEW YORK CITY ICONS

EMPIRE STATE BUILDING

Men of great wealth have a curious habit of building tremendously tall buildings. Perhaps this is a large-scale attempt by these men to leave a mark on the world so that their names will survive after their deaths. It is even more curious, then, that John Jacob Raskob, the General Motors officer and shareholder, did not name his eighty-six-story office building after himself.

Other buildings in the city bore the names of their financers: Chrysler, Woolworth, Chanin. But Raskob gave his building the same name as the state that he wanted to represent: the Empire State Building, the tallest building in the world at the time of completion in 1931. The building sits on the site of the old Waldorf-Astoria and measures 1,250 feet, or eighty-six stories, to the roof. Including two basement floors and the fourteen-story-high spire, there are 102 stories, with a reach of 1,472 feet.

According to the Empire State Building Company, William Lamb, the architect from the firm of Shreve, Lamb, and Harmon, designed the tower based on the simplicity and elegance of a pencil. Indeed, the design does have

The Empire State Building
350 Fifth Avenue
at 34th Street
Manhattan
(212) 736-3100
www.esbnyc.com

a simple, modern elegance to it. And true to Raskob's vision, the building has come to represent both New York City and State. Even after the World Trade Center surpassed the Empire State Building in height, the latter remained the architectural mascot of the city.

The Empire State Building Company even calls the tower an "ambassador to New York," since it has hosted figures such as Fidel Castro, Queen Elizabeth, Prince Charles, Prince Andrew, the Duchess of York, Nikita Khrushchev, and the King of Siam. The building imprints a tangible magnificence on the skyline of the city, and, from the observation deck, provides a panoramic view that stretches into Brooklyn, New Jersey, and New York Bay. It has appeared in *King Kong,* Andy Warhol's *Empire,* Jonathan Safran Foer's *Extremely Loud and Incredibly Close,* and countless other books and films—because a tall building isn't just a tall building, nor is it a glorified headstone for its creators, but something else entirely. It is a testament to architecture, to ambition, to the greatness that all people imagine for themselves, in one form or another.

TIFFANY & CO.

Many know Tiffany & Co. from Truman Capote's 1950 novel *Breakfast at Tiffany's,* or the 1961 film adaptation starring Audrey Hepburn in the lead as Holly Golightly. Or perhaps the narrow demographic of people who were adolescents in 1994 might recognize Tiffany & Co. from a hit single by the band Deep Blue Something.

But the company has earned its own fame, independent of the popular culture that references it. In 1837 Charles Tiffany and John Young established a "stationery and fancy goods emporium" at 259 Broadway. According to the company, they charged fixed prices—a new policy for retail stores of that era—and brought in $4.98 on September 18, their opening day.

In 1853, Charles Tiffany took control of the store, changed the name to Tiffany & Co., and shifted its focus to jewelry. He also hired H. F. Metzler to sculpt the 9-foot figure of Atlas to bear a clock affixed to the storefront—a figure that has come to represent the store, just like its signature blue color. Over the years, Tiffany rose to the top of both

Tiffany & Co.
727 Fifth Avenue
at 57th Street
Manhattan
(212) 755-8000
www.tiffany.com

retail and art circles, setting standards in design, silver quality, technique, and sheer luxury. Abraham Lincoln gave Tiffany jewels to his wife, Mary Todd Lincoln, in 1861; Admiral Farragut, General Grant, and General Sherman received Tiffany presentation swords in 1862; the Boston Museum of Art acquired a Tiffany pitcher in 1873, initiating the company's now widespread presence in museums and collections; in 1885 the company even redesigned the Great Seal of the United States of America, which still exists today on the $1 bill. Tiffany & Co. now has stores around the world, including its flagship store (established 1940) at Fifth Avenue and 57th Street.

Several retailers such as Macy's and FAO Schwarz have reached a level of celebrity uncommon to most commercial enterprises, but Tiffany's is one of the few that has managed to transcend the boundaries of retail and enter the worlds of art, society, and culture. It is one thing to succeed in a particular field, but it is another thing altogether to redefine that field in the process.

TIFFANY & CO.

STATUE OF LIBERTY

Few New Yorkers know the name Charlotte Bartholdi, but every New Yorker knows her face. It is immortalized on the Statue of Liberty, designed by Charlotte's son, French sculptor Frederic-Auguste Bartholdi, and engineered by Gustave Eiffel.

Auguste intended the statue as a gift from the people of France to the people of the United States: a colossal monument to liberty, the ideal both countries valued most. He planned to present Lady Liberty to the American people on July 4, 1876, America's centennial anniversary of independence from England, but pecuniary difficulties caused delays.

A committee called the Union-Franco Amèricaine raised the funds for her from the French people with the aid of Edouard Rene de Laboulaye, the critical statesman and life senator, and Ferdinand de Lesseps, the celebrated diplomat and Suez Canal financer.

Americans were charged with the responsibility of funding and building the statue's pedestal, duties that New Yorkers nearly failed to achieve. Local support for the statue was sparse until

The Statue of Liberty Liberty Island www.nps.gov/stli

The Circle Line operates the ferry to Liberty and Ellis Islands. For ticket prices and schedules, visit www.circle linedowntown .com.

Joseph Pulitzer dedicated himself—and his newspaper, the *New York World*—to the cause. He badgered millionaires and statesmen, but ultimately it was the working class that rose to the task: Readers of the *World* sent pennies and nickels to Pulitzer until he raised $100,000 towards the pedestal. (The last donation, of $250, came from inventor Thomas Edison.)

Unveiled on October 28, 1886, the Statue of Liberty rests on Liberty Island (formerly Bedloe Island). Inside her copper shell and steel framework, visitors can hear the metallic echo of those who believed in the statue and the values for which she stands: Bartholdi, Eiffel, Laboulaye, Lesseps, Pulitzer, the thousands who scraped pennies to fund her, architect Richard Hunt who built the pedestal, and many others.

But it is poet Emma Lazarus who gave the statue its true voice in her poem "The New Colossus," where she describes Lady Liberty as the Mother of Exiles who beckons:
Give me your tired, your poor,
Your huddled masses yearning to breathe free.

BROOKLYN BRIDGE

If bridges could tell stories, the Brooklyn Bridge would talk nonstop for days. It would speak in the reverberant grumble of granite blocks grinding against each other and in the whisper of steel cables. In a long, slow drawl, the bridge would recount the winter of 1852 when it first appeared in the dreams of John Augustus Roebling. It would tell of Roebling's death and the ascendancy of his son, Washington. It would tell of the dozens of men killed during its creation and of the children who grew up during its thirteen years of construction, awestruck by the colossus rising out of the waters of the East River. It would tell how P. T. Barnum crossed the bridge in 1883 with his twenty-one elephants to prove its structural stability, of the thousands of pedestrians who swarmed it during the MTA strike of 2005, of weddings and jumpers and stampedes, of secrets unrecorded anywhere else but in the memory of its stone masonry.

When the Great Bridge opened on May 24, 1883, it was the longest

The Brooklyn Bridge

Manhattan entrance: City Hall at Centre Street

Brooklyn entrance: intersection of Tillary and Adams Streets

For more information, visit the New York City Department of Transportation at www.nyc.gov.

suspension bridge in the world, spanning 1,600 feet between the two towers and over a mile in total. It was also the first steel-cable bridge, a revolutionary concept heralded by John Roebling and completed by his son Washington after his death early in the project. After Washington became housebound due to the decompression sickness, or "the bends," his wife Emily played an essential role as well, serving as an ambassador between him and the bridge's engineers.

The story of the bridge is the story of the Roeblings. It is the story of J. Lloyd Haigh, who sold inferior bridge cables to Roebling for his own profit, and Abram Hewitt, the iron-maker and politician who defended the Roeblings' vision against critics. It is the story of the now-forgotten builders who risked their lives and died during construction, and of the secret vault rediscovered in 2006, filled with provisions during the Cold War in case of a nuclear attack. Oh, if bridges could tell stories, what a story this one would tell!

I ♥ NY

When Milton Glaser designed the I ♥ NY rebus in 1977, he did so pro bono. The New York State Department of Commerce had hired Glaser to design a logo for a statewide marketing campaign (not just for New York City), and Glaser waived the fee, assuming the campaign would be short-lived.

Now, I ♥ NY has become more than a logo or even an icon, but a one-phrase lexicon of sorts. Glaser's original concept has spawned hundreds of parodies and has entered common usage (for example, "I totally heart writers"). It is a symbol, a catchphrase, a T-shirt logo, a tourism ploy. It has been yoked for city pride, state pride, patriotism, and government criticism.

As images often do, the I ♥ NY symbol has outgrown its creator, but Milton Glaser is the most interesting character in its story. He cofounded *New York Magazine* in 1968 along with Clay Felker and served as the president and design director at the magazine until 1977. His own firm, begun in 1974, has produced designs widely viewed throughout the city and the world: the

Milton Glaser Inc.
207 East 32nd
Street at
Third Avenue
Manhattan
(212) 889-3161
http://milton
glaser.com

New York State
Tourism
(800) CALL-NYS
www.iloveny.com

Rainbow Room's graphics, the World Health Organization's International AIDS symbol and poster, the logo for Tony Kushner's play *Angels in America*.

Looking at his body of work, one gets the sense that Glaser is a New York designer—not because he receives so many commissions from New York, but because his career reflects the soul of the city in which he lives. After 9/11, he produced an alternative I ♥ NY logo with the text "I ♥ NY MORE THAN EVER" with a black spot on the heart representing the site of the World Trade Center. He also created the WE ARE ALL AFRICAN poster promoting aid for and awareness of the horrors in Africa. When he addressed the AIGA conference in Boston in 2005, he said: "We can choose how to react to our circumstances. We can reject the passivity and narcissism that leads to despair, and choose to participate in the life of our times." It is because of his dedication to ethics in design that Milton Glaser is an essential component of the I ♥ NY logo—because, essentially, he provides the heart.

CENTRAL PARK

When the state of New York agreed in 1853 to reserve 843 acres of land for the use of Central Park, the parkland was not so central. This was before the Vanderbilts created a mini-metropolis along Park Avenue, back when Midtown didn't mean anything and the middle of town fell somewhere below 14th Street. In 1853, instead of the Chrysler Building, there was Mrs. White's goat farm.

The park was designed by Calvert Vaux and Frederick Law Olmsted—the same man who designed Prospect Park in Brooklyn, the Emerald Necklace in Boston, the Capitol landscape in Washington, D.C., and other well-known spaces throughout North America.

Olmsted and Vaux had different goals for the park. Olmsted took a more dictatorial approach, arguing that the people need to be shown how to use a park, with regulations and park police. Vaux believed that the people who would use the park should help determine its use—that it should be a collaboration between artists, designers, and the public.

Despite these differences, it speaks

Central Park
59th to 110th
Street, Fifth
Avenue to
Central Park
West
Manhattan

Central Park
Conservancy
(212) 310-6600
www.central
parknyc.org

to the foresight of Vaux and Olmsted that the park has changed little in over a century of existence. Bethesda Fountain, completed in 1873 by Emma Stebbins, remains near Central Park Lake. The Central Park menagerie of exotic animals became the Central Park Zoo in 1864 and has remained since. Some things have changed, of course—sheep no longer graze on Sheep Meadow and structures like the Central Park Casino no longer exist—but the overall layout of Vaux and Olmsted's original "Greensward" design still defines the park today.

Like every inch of New York City, Central Park has been subject to various pressures over its lifetime—years of decline, crime, and possible destruction. But in the 1980s, the Central Park Conservancy organization began a highly successful renovation of the park, restoring and maintaining its dilapidated areas and structures. Now the park is experiencing a bit of a renaissance—with Shakespeare in the Park and free concerts and movies during the summer and ice-skating in the winter—harking back to its founders' original dream of a public haven for all.

TIMES SQUARE (NEW YEAR'S EVE)

The New York tradition of assembling in Times Square for New Year's Eve dates back to the birth of Times Square itself. In 1904 the *New York Times* built its headquarters in Longacre Square and convinced the city to rename the square in its honor. At the end of the year, Alfred Ochs, the newspaper's owner, hosted a New Year's Eve celebration in the newly rechristened square, with an all-day street festival and fireworks.

At the end of 1907, when the city banned fireworks from the revelries, Ochs instead hoisted a 700-pound ball made of iron and wood to the top of the New York Times building. Except for 1942 and 1943, when there were wartime power shortages, the ball has dropped from the top of that tower every year since 1907, in its various forms. Over the years, it has grown lighter and brighter—in 1981 through 1988 it even took the shape and coloration of an apple to accompany the city's "I Love New York" campaign.

If space aliens landed on Earth on New Year's Eve and witnessed New

**Times Square
42nd to 48th
Street between
Broadway and
Seventh Avenues
Manhattan**

**Times Square
Alliance
1560 Broadway
Suite 800
Manhattan
(212) 768-1560
www.timessquare
alliance.org**

York's now international celebration, they would probably ask why the new year was heralded with a large, iridescent *ball?* According to the Times Square Alliance, which co-operates the festivities, the concept of a "time ball" dates back to the mid-nineteenth century, when England's Royal Observatory in Greenwich began dropping a ball at one o'clock every afternoon, for the benefit of local ships. Few institutions continue this practice, but the United States Naval Observatory in Washington, D.C., continues to drop a time ball every day at noon.

Grouchy New Yorkers refuse to attend the Times Square event for New Year's Eve, complaining about the crowds and dismissing the whole affair as a glorified tourist attraction. Nevertheless, approximately one million people fill the square every year to witness the ball drop, in a blaze of lights and noise, for that one infinitely small moment when one year ends and another begins, when everyone forgets their work or their woes to kiss each other and dream about the year ahead.

ROCKEFELLER CENTER

The saga of Rockefeller Center has multiple beginnings. Perhaps it began when David Hosack bought the twenty acres of sloped terrain and outcrops of rock from the City of New York in 1801 for just under $5,000. Or maybe it began when the state legislature bought the land back for $75,000 and bequeathed it to Columbia University.

Or perhaps the story really begins on May 21, 1928, at the Metropolitan Club, where the city's wealthiest members met to discuss the financing of a new opera house. The attendees included Marshall Field, Clarence Mackay, Walter Chrysler, Otto Kahn, and a representative of John D. Rockefeller Jr ("Junior"), who supported the acquisition of land from Columbia for the purpose of a new opera house.

Yet the Metropolitan Real Estate Company eventually backed out of the deal and Junior assumed sole responsibility for the project. The story of Junior's acquisition—and the real estate deals that followed throughout the decades—of all the land between 47th and 51st Streets from Fifth to Seventh Avenues could fill a book. And the com-

Rockefeller Center
Fifth to Seventh Avenues between 47th and 51st Streets Manhattan
(212) 332-6868
www.rockefeller center.com

plex of buildings that he completed in 1939 has already filled many books.

From the art deco design of the seventy-story GE Building (formerly the RCA Building) at 30 Rockefeller Plaza to the plentitude of public art, Rockefeller Center has become a menagerie of New York City iconography: Radio City Music Hall, Paul Manship's gilded statue of Prometheus, Lee Lawrie's statue of Atlas, Isamu Noguchi's stainless-steel bas relief, and the annual Rockefeller Christmas tree—not to mention tenants such as Christie's auction house and NBC's television studios.

A $75-million renovation for the observation deck at the top of the GE Building was completed in 2005. Dubbed the Top of the Rock, the observation deck provides a view of Rockefeller Center's elegant symmetry, laid out like an architect's model. It also allows a panoramic view of New York equal to that from the Empire State Building (better, some say, since the view includes Central Park)—where you can see the skyline of the city that the Rockefellers played such a large role in building.

UBS
RADIO CITY MUSIC HALL
RADIO CITY MUSIC HALL
Music Hall RADIO CITY
GUEST PIERS FACCINI SATURDAY, SEPTEMBER 15

HUDSON RIVER

There is something comforting about gravity. It is constant and true. It is what makes a river a river, pulling the water down an elevation gradient like an eager child. And like gravity—like eager children, as well—a river is persistent, following its gradient despite the machinations of humankind along its banks or the dams placed in its way.

New York City rose in a blink of the Hudson's eye. On the timescale of a river, the Hudson is always changing: digging deeper in its channel, altering its course. But on the human timescale, the Hudson has become a comforting constant; from its source at Lake Tear of the Clouds in the Adirondacks through New York Bay and The Narrows to its terminus in the Atlantic.

We have built dams along its route with controversial benefits and damages, and we have, at times, taken the river for granted, as with the notorious dumping of

Hudson River Park Trust (212) 627-2020 www.hudson riverpark.org

Hudson River Foundation (212) 483-7667 www.hudsonriver .org

PCBs (polychlorinated biphenyls) by the General Electric Company beginning in 1946.

New York State and City have in recent years begun to appreciate the river that defines the city's western flank. The state passed its Hazardous Waste Reduction Act in 1989 and created in the 1980s and 1990s the Hudson River Improvement Fund and the New York City Environmental Fund. With the improved health of the estuary and the development of Hudson River Park that began near the year 2000, New Yorkers are again appreciating the constant companionship of the Hudson—the parks, concerts, and events along its shore, its waters for sailing, or its simple scenery. Even more permanent than a statue or a building, the Hudson has become not only a geographical boundary between New York and New Jersey, but a recurring character in the culture of the city.

METROPOLITAN MUSEUM OF ART

The Metropolitan Museum of Art—or, simply, the Met—began only a year after its current neighbor on the Upper West Side, the American Museum of Natural History. Founded in 1870, it originally occupied a building on Fifth Avenue and consisted of three private European collections—174 paintings in total.

In 1880 the Met moved to Central Park, into a building designed by Jacob Mould and Calvert Vaux, the same architects responsible for the original building of the American Museum of Natural History. And like the natural history museum, the Met has since expanded around the original structure. Richard Hunt completed its current beaux-arts facade in 1926, for example, and Kevin Roche John Dinkeloo and Associates performed another extensive architectural overhaul of the museum between 1971 and 1991.

Today the museum houses over two

Metropolitan Museum of Art 1000 Fifth Avenue at 82nd Street Manhattan (212) 535-7710 www.metmuseum .org

The Cloisters 99 Margaret Corbin Drive, Fort Tryon Park Manhattan (212) 923-3700

million works of art that, according to the museum, span 5,000 years of world culture from all over the globe. The building now covers two million square feet and receives 5.2 million visitors every year. Its collections include American, European, Islamic, Asian, and African art, as well as the largest collection of Egyptian art outside of Cairo. It also houses special collections such as arms and armor or costumes.

The museum also operates The Cloisters, a lesser-known New York gem, 9 miles north of the 81st Street main building. The Cloisters occupies a site in Fort Tryon Park in upper Manhattan that consists of twelfth- through fifteenth-century architecture. It displays art and architecture from medieval Europe—although many visitors who don't have an interest in medieval tapestries still visit the site for its monastic gardens and serene setting.

FAO SCHWARZ

FAO Schwarz, one of New York's most visited retailers, began not in New York but in Baltimore, Maryland. Frederick August Otto Schwarz and his three brothers opened a toy shop in 1862, selling European-style toys such as china-headed dolls and wooden playhouses.

FAO Schwarz
767 Fifth Avenue
at 58th Street
Manhattan
(212) 644-9400
www.faoschwarz
.com

The brothers later spread out like the sons of Jacob and founded toy bazaars in Philadelphia, Boston, and New York, in addition to the original Baltimore store. Around 1870 Frederick Schwarz opened his New York bazaar, eventually to be named FAO Schwarz.

The store grew in notoriety, and as the city migrated north, so did the FAO Schwarz storefront, until it landed at its current location at the corner of 58th Street and Fifth Avenue in 1986.

Just like retailers in Times Square, the FAO Schwarz store made its reputation not just on its toys but on the experience, as captured in the 1988 film *Big*, in which Tom Hanks and Robert Loggia play "Chopsticks" on a 22-foot piano keyboard spread out on the floor. Coincidentally, the FAO Schwarz experience revolves around making everything big: the oversized keyboard, a three-story clock tower, colossal Lego structures, and life-size stuffed animals.

Despite strategic and financial difficulty for the FAO Schwarz chain after 2000, the company has reorganized and recovered. New York's flagship store remains at its Fifth Avenue location by the southeast corner of Central Park and remains a popular draw for New Yorkers and visitors alike.

THE WALDORF-ASTORIA HOTEL

Nineteenth-century millionaire William Waldorf Astor lived in the Empire State Building. Or, rather, he lived in a mansion on Fifth Avenue at 33rd Street, the future site of the city's most characteristic skyscraper.

William Astor inherited the legendary Astor fortune when his father, John Jacob Astor III, died in 1890. The surviving Astor decided to raze his father's residence on Fifth Avenue and raise a grand hotel in its place—the Waldorf Hotel. Designed by Henry Hardenbergh to boast every modern convenience imaginable, such as electricity in every room and private guest bathrooms, the Waldorf opened on March 24, 1893. In 1897 Astor's cousin John Jacob Astor IV constructed the Astoria Hotel on the lot adjacent to the Waldorf. A corridor built between them gave birth to the Waldorf-Astoria Hotel.

In 1929 the owners of the hotel agreed to destroy it to make way for the construction of the Empire State Build-

The Waldorf-Astoria Hotel
301 Park Avenue
at 49th Street
Manhattan
(212) 355-3000
http://waldorf astoria.hilton .com

ing. They relocated to 301 Park Avenue, where the Waldorf-Astoria reemerged in 1931, larger and even more luxurious. Designed by the architectural firm of Leonard Schultze and S. Fullerton Weaver, the new beaux-arts hotel rose forty-seven stories—the largest hotel of the time.

Many new concepts in the operation of hotels began at the Waldorf-Astoria: room service, the abolition of sexual segregation, and, strangely, a salad. On the site of the first Waldorf Hotel, the maître d'hôtel Oscar Tschirky (also known as "Oscar of the Waldorf") supposedly created the Waldorf salad: a combination of apples, celery, and mayonnaise. Later, the recipe incorporated walnuts and lettuce.

So this is the legacy of William Waldorf Astor and his cousin John Jacob Astor IV: a landmarked hotel known throughout the world, a reputation as one of New York City's founding families, and a salad.

YELLOW TAXI

On May 20, 1899, Jacob German, a taxi driver for the Electric Vehicle Company, sped down Lexington Avenue at 12 miles per hour. A patrolman on a bicycle witnessed German driving at this "breakneck" speed and made him the first person in New York history to get a speeding ticket.

The history of the taxicab does not begin with the horse-drawn hansom cabs that preceded automobiles or the advent of the taximeter used to measure distances. It begins with Jacob German's speeding ticket, the first example of the double-sided nature of taxi drivers' notorious reputations: On one hand, they are the hardworking immigrant class of New York, diligently hustling for fares; on the other hand, they are reckless madmen behind the wheel.

In 1937 Mayor Fiorello LaGuardia created the medallion system that limits the number of taxis allowed to operate in the city. And thirty years later, in 1967, the city ordered all medallion cabs to be painted yellow, reportedly to cut down on the number of rogue cabs operating without medallions. Today there are nearly 13,000 taxi cabs in the

The New York Taxi & Limousine Commission 40 Rector Street at the West Side Highway Manhattan (212) NEW-YORK or 311 within the five boroughs www.nyc.gov

city and about 40,000 drivers.

While the yellow color of taxis makes them iconic, it is the drivers themselves who make them legendary. Every New Yorker has a taxi story. It is a rite of passage like a bar mitzvah or communion. There is the enraged driver who aims for bicyclists, or the late-night driver who takes a young girl from the Bronx to New Jersey for free. Drivers can be sleazy, smelly, honest, talkative, safe, or maniacal—and despite the city's fines for cell-phone use while driving or its regulation on incense, a taxi ride will always be an adventure.

Taxi drivers must have stories to tell as well. The average driver serves a twelve-hour shift, driving 180 miles and picking up thirty fares. They ferry children to birthday parties, executives to meetings, and couples making out in the backseat to nowhere in particular. They are the city's secret-bearers, witnessing scandals, chaste romances, adultery, historic business meetings, impromptu song-singing, anniversaries, and deaths. We can romanticize them or demonize them, but without them, where would we be?

YANKEE STADIUM
AND SHEA STADIUM

In 1919 the New York Yankees bought Babe Ruth from the Boston Red Sox, which changed everything. The Yankees transformed from a mediocre franchise to one of the best in the American League while the Red Sox fell into an eighty-six-year losing streak.

In 1921 the National League's New York Giants expelled the Yankees from the Polo Grounds where both teams had previously played. The Yankees' owners decided to build their own stadium— the first baseball arena to be called a stadium, in fact—across the Harlem River in the Bronx. This stadium included three tiers of seating in the grandstand and sat on ten acres of land bought for $675,000.

The Yankees' team roster has included some of the most famous names in baseball: Babe Ruth, Lou Gehrig, Joe DiMaggio, Mickey Mantle, Whitey Ford, Yogi Berra, Roger Maris, Derek Jeter and Alex Rodriguez. Yet the team has puttered through lackluster periods of moderate success, much like the stadium itself, which has suffered periods of deterioration followed by multimillion-dollar renovations and the latest plan

Yankee Stadium
161st Street at
River Avenue
Bronx
(718) 293-4300
http://newyork
.yankees.mlb
.com

Shea Stadium
123-01 Roosevelt
Avenue, at
126th Street
Queens
(718) 507-METS
http://newyork
.mets.mlb.com

to build a new stadium adjacent to the current one.

There is another pair of stadiums— one retiring and one newly forming—9 miles away, in Flushing, Queens. Shea Stadium opened in 1964 to host the newly formed New York Mets of the National League, and its successor, Citi Field, is slated to open adjacent to Shea in 2009.

If the New York Yankees are the story of glory sometimes tarnished by misfortune, the New York Mets are the story of misfortune sometimes uplifted by glory. Baseball journalists have called the team lovable losers and the worst team that money can buy, and their 1969 and 1986 World Series titles are widely considered underdog wins.

The difficult question: *Are you a Mets fan or a Yankees fan?* gets at the root of a person. It depends only a little on the borough where you grew up, and much more on what you believe. Do you believe in the underdog or the top dog? Faith or fact? Do you love baseball for the passion of the game or for the glory? Do you believe in the Mets or the Yankees?

CARNEGIE HALL

Carnegie Hall began, according to its current owners, on a ship named *Fulda* in the spring of 1887. It was the meeting of three passengers onboard the ship that gave birth to the hall: Walter Damrosch, the young conductor and musical director of the Symphony Society of New York and the Oratorio Society of New York, Andrew Carnegie, the steel baron and philanthropist, and his new bride, Louise Whitfield, a former Oratorio Society soprano. This confluence of characters reads like basic arithmetic: ambitious conductor + millionaire philanthropist + musically inclined wife = Carnegie Hall.

The hall opened in 1891 as the Music Hall founded by Andrew Carnegie and owed much of its immediate success to the design of architect William Tuthill. The official opening of the concert hall included performances by the Symphony Society and the Oratorio Society, under the direction of Damrosch and Pyotr Ilyich Tchaikovsky (the Russian composer best known for his *Swan Lake Suite*).

Since its auspicious beginning, the hall was renamed Carnegie Hall and has

*Carnegie Hall
881 Seventh
Avenue at
56th Street
 Manhattan
Box office:
(212) 247-7800
Administration:
(212) 903-9600
www.carnegie
hall.org*

hosted the greatest figures of classical music, from composers like Philip Glass to violinists like Itzhak Perlman. When comedian Red Skelton performed in 1977, he said, "If I had known it would be like this, I would have studied the violin."

It's impossible to list the juggernauts of talent that have performed on the Carnegie stage, for their numbers are legion—and not limited to classical music. The venue hosts all varieties of music and performance: anything, really, that will fit on its stage. And the procession of figures who have shared that stage—The Beatles, The Rolling Stones, Vladimir Horowitz, the New York Philharmonic, Nina Simone, Count Basie, Jack London, Emmeline Pankhurst, Margaret Sanger, Winston Churchill, Mark Twain, Booker T. Washington—have made Carnegie Hall a fantasy for any performer. To appear on the Carnegie Hall stage, just for one night, has become the ultimate mark of success. This is why Arthur Rubinstein, when asked in the street how to get to Carnegie Hall, replied: "Practice, practice, practice."

BAGEL/BIALY

The bagel is an icon of New York City as spaghetti is an icon of Italy: They have both become ubiquitous outside of their iconographic homes. People all over the country speak wistfully of the quintessential New York bagel—found at every corner deli in the city and well-known shops such as H&H or Murray's. But the bagel has a lesser-known sibling, one virtually undiscovered outside of the city: the bialy, a breakfast roll that emigrated from eastern Europe in the late nineteenth century, at the same time as the bagel.

Unlike the bagel, the bialy is not boiled before baking, and where the bagel has an ostentatious hole, the bialy has a modest indent, often filled with diced onions, seeds, garlic, or herbs. Although the bialy is more breadlike than the bagel, it proves just as delicious with a schmear of cream cheese and an inch of lox.

The bialy takes its name from Bialystok, Poland, the same city that lends its name to the Bialystoker Synagogue, a monolith of Lower East Side Jewry originally built in 1826. Just 5 blocks away from the synagogue is Kossar's Bialys,

Kossar's Bialys (and bagels) 367 Grand Street at Essex Street Manhattan (877) 4-BIALYS www.kossars bialys.com

the long-standing holy land of bialy bakeries.

Bagels, on the other hand, have a less clear origin. The most common explanation posits that an Austrian baker made a bagel in the shape of a stirrup for Jan Sobieski, the King of Poland, in honor of his military victory over the Turks in 1683. Two centuries later the massive emigration from eastern Europe would introduce the bagel and bialy to North America (where cream cheese originated in 1872, in New York State).

While the bagel has migrated from New York across North America, the bialy has remained a dedicated New Yorker. The bialy's introversion does not stem from a lack of sensory appeal, however. Just walk along Grand Street at two in the morning when Kossar's bakes its bialys. Stand outside the door, where flour dust mingles with the earthen smell of baking bread and rising dough, cut by the acrid tang of onions. Ask the baker for a fresh bialy right out of the oven—hold it carefully like a hot potato, blow on it, take a bite, and know that this is New York City.

NEW YORK NEWSPAPERS

New York City's first newspaper was the *New York Gazette,* founded by William Bradford in 1725. The city's second newspaper, however, earned more notoriety. The *New York Weekly Journal,* founded by John Zenger in 1733, broke free from the journalistic trend of the day of avoiding political criticism. Zenger, however, published articles criticizing New York's governor William Crosby. Crosby arrested Zenger for seditious libel in 1734, but at the subsequent trial the jury found Zenger innocent.

Some publications have continued in Zenger's spirit of dedication to journalistic objectivity and integrity. Publisher Adolph Ochs purchased the *New York Times* in 1896, and began the process that has established it as one of the most respectable newspapers in the world. (Incidentally, the current publisher of the *Times* is Arthur Ochs Sulzberger Jr., a descendent of Adolph Ochs.) The *Wall Street Journal,* founded by Dow Jones & Company in 1889, sits with the *Times* as one of the finest—and most circulated—newspapers in the United States.

Rupert Murdoch's News Corporation bought the *Wall Street Journal* in May 2007, raising concerns that he would sacrifice the paper's reputation in order to enforce his own agenda. Murdoch also owns the *New York Post,* founded by Alexander Hamilton in 1801. Both the *Post* and the *New York Daily News,* launched in 1919, are tabloid newspapers, competing with each other to cover celebrity gossip and sensational news stories.

Whether respectable or entertaining, New York publications are proliferate: the *New Yorker, New York Magazine,* the *Village Voice,* the *Forward,* the *Epoch Times,* the *Brooklyn Daily Eagle.* The city is also the book-publishing capital of the United States, not to mention the legions of other media outlets, from broadcast to the Web. Every writer, singer, musician, filmmaker, editor, or producer with grandiose ambitions will eventually land in New York City. Whether you are a realist or an idealist, a Murdoch or an Ochs, New York City is your soapbox. Climb up, speak your mind, and hope that someone out there is listening.

WASHINGTON SQUARE PARK

It's a strange coincidence that Washington Square Park, one of New York's busiest and most well-known public spaces, began as a cemetery. In 1797 the Common Council of New York bought land on what is now Washington Square Park for a public cemetery warranted by the yellow fever epidemic. (To this day, there are still more than 20,000 bodies underneath the square.) Since the city bought the land, it has served several purposes: a dueling grounds, a site for public hangings, a military parade ground, and finally, a park.

The fountain, one of the park's two distinctive features, was completed in 1852, although modified later. The second distinctive feature is the Washington Square Arch, completed in 1892 and designed by architect Standford White after the Arc de Triomphe in Paris. This marble version of the arch replaced a previous wooden version from 1889 that celebrated the 100th anniversary of George Washington's inauguration. The two statues of Wash-

Washington Square Park Bounded by University Place, West 4th Street, MacDougal Street, and Waverly Place Manhattan

ington that adorn the northern face of the arch, one of him as president and one as commander in chief, were added later, in 1918.

The park has witnessed many famous events such as marches for labor rights, the women's suffrage parade of 1915, and countless graduations of New York University. It has also hosted several celebrities, before and after they entered the public eye: Willa Cather, Upton Sinclair, Marcel Duchamp, Allen Ginsberg, and Bob Dylan. It has served as a central location for the cultural movements that have characterized the Chelsea neighborhood such as the Beat Generation and the hippie movement. As such, it has also appeared in numerous popular-culture references: *Washington Square* by Henry James and the films *When Harry Met Sally* and *Searching for Bobby Fischer,* for example. Today it still serves as a principal location of New York City amalgamation, where musicians, chess players, students, businesspeople, sword fighters, lovers, and poets all jumble together.

NEW YORK PUBLIC LIBRARY

If Grand Central is the heart of New York City, then the public library is its brain. It is strange, then, that the city didn't have a fully public library until 1911, when cities such as Boston, Philadelphia, and Washington, D.C., all had libraries by the turn of the century.

Before 1911 the city did have semi-public libraries, however: those of Jacob Astor and James Lenox. It was the combined collections and financial resources of these two libraries, along with a gift of $2.4 million from former governor Samuel Tilden, that provided the foundation for the New York Public Library.

The city built the main library building, which is now the Humanities and Social Sciences research library, on Fifth Avenue and 42nd Street, on the site of the Croton Reservoir. The library system now includes four research libraries and eighty-six branch libraries throughout Manhattan, Staten Island, and the Bronx (Queens and Brooklyn have their own separate library systems). In fact, the branch libraries began

The New York Public Library
Fifth Avenue and 42nd Street
Manhattan
(212) 930-0800
www.nypl.org

due to the philanthropy of another New York giant, Andrew Carnegie, who donated $5.2 million for the purpose.

And yet the library is not known worldwide for its vast system of operation or for its eleven million items in the branch and research libraries—not even for the beaux-arts design of the Humanities and Social Sciences building or its famous reading room—but for the two lions who sit outside this building. Sculpted by Edward Clark Potter out of pink Tennessee marble, the lions have guarded the gates of New York's intellectual inheritance ever since the library's dedication on May 23, 1911. They have received several nicknames that have faded over the years: Leo Astor and Leo Lenox, after two of the founders; and later, Patience and Fortitude, the two qualities that Mayor LaGuardia wished for New Yorkers during the trials of the Great Depression in the 1930s. The library has even adopted a lion's head as its logo, reproduced on 1.86 million library cards throughout the city.

BRONX ZOO

The Bronx Zoo covers 265 acres of land in Bronx Park, adjacent to the botanical garden and Fordham University (the university, in fact, sold the parkland to the city for $1 for the construction of a zoo and a garden). With over 4,000 animals, the zoo is considered one of the largest in North America.

The zoo opened its doors on November 8, 1899, under the direction of the New York Zoological Society, for the purpose of zoological study, wildlife conservation, and public education. The zoo has a long history of nurturing endangered species, such as the work of former director William T. Hornaday to rebuild populations of American bison. As the numbers of bison dwindled in the American West, Hornaday bred herds at the Bronx Zoo and in 1907 returned fifteen of them to Oklahoma's Wichita Mountain

*The Wildlife
Conservation
Society
2300 Southern
Boulevard
at 182nd Street
Bronx
(718) 220-5100
www.bronxzoo
.com*

Preserve. Later transfers established bison in Montana, South Dakota, and Nebraska, and the survival of bison today is in large part because of Hornaday's efforts.

The New York Zoological Society became the Wildlife Conservation Society (WCS) in 1993 and maintained its dedication to species diversity. Recently, for example, the WCS helped secure South Brother Island, a seven-acre plot in the East River, half a mile from the Bronx shore, as a sanctuary for egrets, cormorants, and night herons.

The zoo itself features exhibits like the Congo Gorilla Forest, Himalayan Highlands Habitat, an indoor Asian rain forest, and World of Birds. In addition to the Bronx Zoo, the WCS operates the Central Park Zoo, Queens Zoo, Prospect Park Zoo, and New York Aquarium.

MUSEUM OF MODERN ART

John D. Rockefeller Jr. hated modern art. His wife, Abby Aldrich Rockefeller, however, did not. Although John loathed the idea of a museum for modern art, Abby created one with independent funds and the help of her friends Miss Lillie P. Bliss and Mrs. Cornelius J. Sullivan. They founded the Museum of Modern Art in 1929, with an initial gift of eight prints and one drawing.

John eventually supported the museum with various gifts, including its current site on 53rd Street between Fifth and Sixth Avenues, and the Rockefeller family remains intimately involved with the museum, with funding from the Rockefellers Brothers Fund and two members of the family on the board of trustees.

The museum has undergone several reincarnations since its

The Museum of Modern Art
11 West 53rd Street between Fifth and Sixth Avenues
Manhattan
(212) 708-9400
www.moma.org

modest beginnings, most recently the new MoMA designed by Yoshio Taniguchi, opened to the public in stages in 2004 and 2006. The museum now houses 150,000 paintings, sculptures, drawings, prints, photographs, architectural models and drawings, and design objects—from the art world's best-known names to the least known.

The museum also has an exclusive partnership with P.S. 1, an art museum in Queens (which hosts summer dance parties every Saturday that draw revelers from all five boroughs). Along with the holdings of P.S. 1 and MoMA's extensive research, education, and archive materials, MoMA has become, as Abby Rockefeller and her friends originally intended, not just a museum devoted to modern art, but an institution.

CHRYSLER BUILDING

Claudia Pierpont noted in the *New Yorker* that the Chrysler Building wouldn't exist if the Coney Island amusement park Dreamland hadn't burned down. William H. Reynolds, the entrepreneur connected to the corrupt government of Tammany Hall, had opened Dreamland in 1904 as a competitor to the popular Luna Park. When a fire broke out in 1911, appropriately at the Hell's Gate exhibit, and razed the entire lot, Reynolds chose not to rebuild and instead turned his speculating eye towards Manhattan.

Reynolds wanted to join the race for the tallest building in the world and leased the site of the future Chrysler Building from Cooper Union. He drew up plans for the tower, but then sold his interests to Walter Chrysler, who was looking to build a headquarters for his automobile empire. Chrysler and architect William Van Alen reworked Reynolds' comparatively conservative design, emerging with a masterpiece that would

Chrysler Building
405 Lexington
Avenue at
43rd Street
Manhattan
(212) 682-3070

become one of the most cited examples of art deco architecture. The building incorporated several aesthetic features from the cars that funded its construction: the eagles on the sixty-first floor replicate Chrysler hood ornaments of the 1920s, and radiator cap replicas adorn the thirty-first floor.

Completed on May 27, 1930, the Chrysler building spent 339 days as the tallest building in the world, until the Empire State Building opened on May 1, 1931. The Chrysler Building rose seventy-seven floors, was 1,048 feet high, and required 29,961 tons of steel, 3,826,000 bricks, and cost about $20,000,000. Even though the Empire State Building surpassed the Chrysler in height, the Chrysler continues to draw tourists for aesthetic reasons that the Empire never could: the art deco design, sculptural motifs, murals, and three-story triangular lobby built out of red Moroccan marble, onyx, blue marble, and steel.

MACY'S
THANKSGIVING DAY PARADE

Thanksgiving is turkey. It is pumpkin pie. It is your uncle Melvin in a ridiculous Pilgrim costume. And it is the Macy's Thanksgiving Day Parade. Even if you grew up without a television set, you are familiar with the procession of floats and balloons that marches from 77th Street and Central Park West to Herald Square. You can call it the Macy's Parade, the Thanksgiving Parade, or just the Parade, but everyone will know what you're talking about.

According to Macy's, the parade began in 1924 when a group of Macy's employees, most of them second-generation Americans, wanted to celebrate this American holiday with a festival reminiscent of the ones in Europe. Employees dressed in costumes and marched through the city with lions, tigers, and bears from the Central Park Zoo. The parade's famous balloons didn't enter the parade until 1927, with Felix the Cat.

Over the years, the parade grew and grew, every year with a cast of clas-

The Macy's Thanksgiving Day Parade
(212) 494-4495
www.macys.com

Visitor Center
810 Seventh Avenue at 52nd Street Manhattan
(212) 494-2922
www.nycvisit.com

sic characters and the introduction of new ones. Before 1997 the average balloon was six stories high. The Yogi Bear balloon, for example, took 400 yards of nylon and thirty gallons of paint to make. Superman, the largest balloon ever built for the parade, required 14,000 cubic feet of helium and air.

The wind and rain have caused some trouble for the parade, with recent accidents in 1993, 1997, and 2005—which spurred greater safety rules, such as the elimination of the larger balloons. However, this doesn't stop over 2.5 million people from lining the 2.5 mile route every year, in wind, rain, or sun. Many adults have outgrown the characters of their childhood such as Big Bird, Snoopy, Kermit the Frog, and Bullwinkle the moose. And yet there is something wonderful about a six-story yellow bird floating through the streets of Manhattan that can make us all feel like children again, at least for one afternoon.

ETHNIC CUISINE

Sushi, knishes, dumplings, lasagna, falafel, kielbasa, hot dogs, pastrami, potato pancakes, gelato, curry, pad thai, pho, matzo ball soup, Jamaican patties, coco bread, crepes, cannoli, hummus, tabouleh, kimchi. Not all cities can boast as complete a spectrum of ethnic foods as New York.

The former seat of immigration into the United States, New York has assimilated people from almost every country in the world. While these groups—the German and eastern European Jews, Italians, Irish, Chinese, Dominican—have formed different enclaves throughout the city, it is their foods that define them.

In fact, you could probably recognize different neighborhoods blindfolded, just by following your nose. If you smell the subtle aroma of hops and crisp french fries, you're probably walking past the Irish pubs of Woodside, Queens. The powerful wafts of spiced meats and fried plantains drift through the Caribbean neighborhood of Flatbush, Brooklyn. The alternating odors of sharp cheeses, olives, and spinach pie mark the Greek neighborhood of Astoria, Queens. And if you walk along Mott Street in Manhattan's Little Italy you'll stumble upon Di Palo Fine Foods, where they make their own silken white balls of buffalo mozzarella.

Every culture in New York has its own cuisine, which, in a way, is what the many cultures of New York have in common: a strong historical bond with food. In all of these cultures, food is not just food. Cooking is how a mother says "I love you" to a son, how mourners care for each other after a death, how we celebrate a birthday or a holiday. Food is a currency, a language, a basic need, and an art. That is why, when people discuss the diverse cultures of New York City, the first thing they will mention is the food.

BROADWAY

Broadway has two faces. The first face belongs to the road itself that runs north–south from the tip of Manhattan at Bowling Green through the city all the way to Westchester County.

Plenty of New York landmarks sit along Broadway—Trinity Church, Union Square, Lincoln Center, Juilliard, Zabar's, Columbia University—but it is Times Square that gives the avenue its other face. The square and the surrounding theater district lend Broadway its international reputation as the center for American theater.

Strangely, only four theaters exist with proper Broadway addresses. The rest huddle close to the avenue on the east–west streets between 41st and 53rd. That 12-block stretch of Broadway instead hosts the circus of Times Square, with its unyielding bombardment of billboards and flashing lights. (It is the impressive electrical lighting, since the erection of the New York Times building in 1904, that gave Broadway the nickname "the Great White Way.")

As the anchor of the theater district, Broadway has become the Hollywood of stage acting—where aspiring actors

Ticketmaster
Broadway
(212) 307-4100 or
(800) 755-4000
www.ticket
master.com
/broadway

pray for a big break or where established actors groom their careers. The history of theater on Broadway dates back to the nineteenth century, when New York City spread northward from the original settlements on the southern tip of Manhattan. Theaters and theater culture grew robust, exemplified by the success of Edwin Booth's Players Club, founded in 1888 on the border of Gramercy Park.

The area transitioned through theater, vaudeville, and burlesque, and eventually became the city's red-light district in the 1960s and 1970s. In the 1980s, however, a combined effort from the city and private enterprise (such as Disney, which leased the New Amsterdam Theater on 42nd Street) led to a revitalization of the area—albeit a controversial one. Some New Yorkers approved of a cleaner Times Square but not at the cost of Disneyfication.

Today Broadway remains New York's central artery. It is the monarch of American theater, one of the city's oldest avenues, and the mecca of shopping in neighborhoods like SoHo or Midtown, attracting millions of tourists and natives alike.

CIRCLE LINE

Before 1895, Spuyter Duyvil Creek, which connected the Hudson and Harlem Rivers, ran north of the Marble Hill neighborhood, completely separating Manhattan from the Bronx. In 1895, however, the city dug the Harlem River Ship Canal south of Marble Hill, making the neighborhood a temporary island until it filled the creek in 1914. (Marble Hill is now the only neighborhood of Manhattan disconnected from the island itself.)

The opening of the Harlem River Ship Canal spurred a new craze for pleasure cruises around Manhattan. Several competing tourist companies emerged in the early twentieth century, several of which merged in 1945 to form the Circle Line company—including those

*Circle Line
Pier 83 at West
42nd Street
Manhattan
(212) 563-3200
www.circleline
.com*

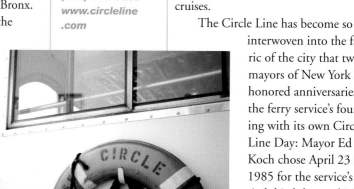

of Frank Berry and Joe Moran. Today the Circle Line is the ferry service that operates the Statue of Liberty and Ellis Island routes, in addition to its harbor cruises.

The Circle Line has become so interwoven into the fabric of the city that two mayors of New York have honored anniversaries of the ferry service's founding with its own Circle Line Day: Mayor Ed Koch chose April 23 in 1985 for the service's fortieth birthday, and Mayor Rudolph Giuliani selected June 15 in 1995 for its fiftieth. Like the Staten Island Ferry, the Circle Line even came to the city's aid in its moment of need: It ceased regular ferry service on September 11, 2001, to transport people out of the city into New Jersey.

GRANT'S TOMB

The tomb of Ulysses S. Grant and his wife, Julia, squats quietly on the Upper West Side of Manhattan, shrouded by trees and eclipsed by Riverside Church. Like the man himself, Grant's tomb has faded from the memory of many New Yorkers; the twin granite sarcophagi inside draw a consistent but modest stream of visitors. But it is the largest mausoleum in North America, which makes one wonder . . . who was Ulysses S. Grant?

Historians remember Grant (born Hiram Ulysses Grant) as many men: the distinguished and prescient lieutenant of the Mexican War, Civil War hero, humble president of the United States, a man of tremendous success, and a man of equally tremendous failure. And few historians manage to consolidate these disparate personas into one man. The biographer William McFeely, however, writes that the story of Grant is "a story of the quest of an ordinary American man in the mid-nineteenth century to make his mark."

Perhaps the greatness of Grant stems from the fact that he was not

General Grant National Memorial 122nd Street and Riverside Drive www.nps.gov/gegr

particularly great: He was a man just like any other, from a family of variable success and an unexceptional upbringing. Yet he rose through the ranks of the military, until he commanded the entire Union Army during the Civil War. After the forced surrender of Robert E. Lee in 1865, Grant rode this wave of success to the White House in 1868, where he served as president through 1876.

And perhaps Americans remember Grant so fondly—despite his failures as a president, despite his great disappointment to black Americans and his post-presidential downfall—because he was a mostly typical man who left an entirely atypical mark on the world. Underneath the various ambitions of men and women, beneath our dreams of wealth or fame or sacrifice, isn't this what we all strive for—to make our lives significant?

"If his presidency, crooked as a dog's hind leg, tarnished Grant's historical standing, it certainly hasn't diminished his hold on popular affections."
—Richard Norton Smith

ELLIS ISLAND

No one ever wanted Ellis Island. Originally, it was just a slurry of mud and clay, inhabited only by seagulls—a meager two or three acres of land that barely poked above the waterline of New York Bay. After the colonial government of New Amsterdam bought the island in 1630 and dubbed it Oyster Island, this undesirable protrusion in New York Bay changed ownership and names multiple times—even serving, under the name Gibbet Island, as an execution site for condemned criminals.

The federal government acquired the island indirectly from the estate of Samuel Ellis—who gave his name to the brackish swath—in 1808. By the early 1900s, the government had expanded the island using landfill from the excavation for Grand Central Station and converted the once unpopulated island into the processing center for millions of immigrants to the United States.

The island processed immigrants between 1892 and 1954, and now serves as an immigration museum, including the original, restored buildings.

But the story of Ellis Island is not

The Statue of Liberty–Ellis Island Foundation, Inc. (212) 561-4588 www.ellisisland.org

the story of its many owners and speculators, nor is it about the pirates who hung there for their crimes. Rather, the story of Ellis Island encompasses the stories of each of the twelve million people who passed through its doors: the Lithuanian woman sent back across the Atlantic because she had trachoma; the Guadalupean sisters who arrived separately to the United States and found each other again; the Finnish families, the Russian families, the Montenegrins, Scandinavians, Chinese, Irish, Jewish, Catholic, Muslim, Buddhist—even Bob Hope, Charlie Chaplin, and Isaac Asimov.

It is said that one in four Americans is descended from an immigrant who passed through Ellis Island. That is why the island's story will never fit on this page—or any number of pages, for that matter. It is too many stories—individual hopes and terrors that fertilized the country as we know it today. The island is no longer a mass of land and buildings, but twelve million different memories—twelve million beginnings, or middles, or endings, depending on how you see it.

GRAND CENTRAL

The first wonder of Grand Central Terminal is the sheer marvel of its architecture and art: the facade with its three great portals; the massive sculptural group of Mercury, Hercules, and Minerva; and the majestic Main Concourse with its astrological ceiling.

The second wonder of Grand Central is that it still exists at all.

Originally built by railroad tycoon Cornelius Vanderbilt as Grand Central Depot in 1871, the site underwent several reconstructions, first as Grand Central Station and finally as Grand Central Terminal in 1913. This final reincarnation involved extensive excavation of the train yards, as the railroad industry transitioned to electrical power. The train yard—once acres of tracks and belching locomotives—was submerged underground and paved over, giving birth to the concept of "air rights": the valuable real estate above the tracks was leased, giving rise to the modern metropolis of Park Avenue.

But the glory of Grand Central declined along with the general waning of the railroad industry. By the

Grand Central Terminal
42nd Street and
Park Avenue
http://grand
centralterminal
.com

1950s the station was reporting losses of $24 million per year. In 1963 demolition began on another losing railroad venture, Penn Station. Subsequently, developers and agencies ratcheted up pressure to submit Grand Central to a similar fate.

Two events saved Grand Central from destruction: the Landmarks Preservation Commission designated the exterior of Grand Central as a landmark; and a 1978 Supreme Court decision upheld that landmark status, which proved a key turning point for preservation efforts nationwide.

Now Grand Central has been restored to its former glory and enhanced with a shopping center and restaurants. About 125,000 commuters and 500,000 visitors pass through the terminal every day. The station has witnessed the rise of New York. It has ushered soldiers to and from two world wars; housed countless homeless people during financial crises; and silently observed the lives of millions of New Yorkers, who continue to pass through its exalted gates.

JUNIOR'S CHEESECAKE

To understand the nostalgic appeal of Junior's cheesecake, you first have to understand what an egg cream is. An egg cream consists of chocolate syrup, seltzer water, and milk—although it did include eggs and cream in the early 1900s, before World War II.

Egg creams evoke classic, rough-and-tumble Brooklyn. They come from the same New York epoch as soda fountains in drugstores, stickball in the streets, the rise of skyscrapers on the Manhattan skyline, and the Great Depression. In the era of the egg cream, the Dodgers baseball team still hailed from Brooklyn.

It is this era from which Junior's was born. Harry Rosen, whose family owned a diner at the corner of Flatbush and DeKalb Avenues since 1929, opened Junior's at that

Junior's
86 Flatbush
Avenue Extension
at DeKalb Avenue
Brooklyn
(718) 852-5257
www.juniors
cheesecake.com

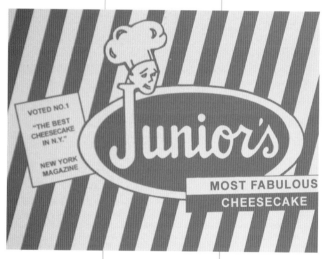

location in 1950. In addition to serving hamburgers and egg creams like any other diner, Rosen worked with baker Eigel Peterson to develop a distinctive cheesecake recipe that Junior's would come to market as "the world's most famous cheesecake."

Whether the marketing campaign preceded the popularity of Junior's cheesecake or vice-a-versa doesn't really matter. Junior's now sells cheesecakes all over the country and has stores in Grand Central Station and Times Square. So even if you don't remember old-time New York or share romanticized versions of the early twentieth century, you can still enjoy Junior's restaurant. All you need is a love for creamy, spongy, makes-you-do-cartwheels-in-the-street cheesecake.

DIAMOND DISTRICT

Storefronts overflow with diamonds and precious gems, reflecting and refracting the sunlight into the street and back towards the sky. Couples hold hands and peer in the windows, occasionally pointing at a particular ring or necklace. Armored cars line the streets, and customers, tourists, brokers, and sellers pack the sidewalks.

Hasidic Jews, mostly men in their distinctively long, black suits, with stiff fedoras on their heads and ringlets hanging from their temples, bustle between shops and offices, buying and selling from each other, haggling over interest rates or returned goods, and sealing every deal with a handshake. The Jewish diaspora has held an important role in the international diamond business for centuries, and after World War II, increased Jewish immigration to the United States caused a massive upswing in New York's gem trade. Spurred by this growth, the already existing Diamond Dealer's Club moved to 47th Street in the 1940s and thus began the Diamond District as it exists today.

Tourists and customers don't see the offices behind or above the shops,

The Diamond District
47th Street between Fifth and Sixth Avenues Manhattan

47th Street Business Improvement District (212) 302-5739 www.diamond district.org

but it is these hidden spaces where much of the district's transactions occur. Ninety percent of diamonds bought in the United States reportedly pass through New York City, primarily through these back offices where brokers buy and sell gems. The district brings in $400 million in gross income on an average day, placing it among the world's primary centers for gem trading, along with Johannesburg, Antwerp, and London. As such, diamonds connect New York to the politics and economies of countries around the world. From political unrest in Sierra Leone, Angola, and the Democratic Republic of Congo, to the economic stability of South Africa, to the fortune of the Oppenheimer family controlling the De Beers cartel, to the unofficial fortunes of smugglers, revolutionaries, and guerillas who profit from black-market trade.

These global interactions and clashes of cultures, governments, and businesspeople, all come together here, in the storefronts of 47th Street, with their glittering wares spread out for customers to ogle and, the merchants hope, to purchase.

LINCOLN CENTER

Lincoln Center began, like much of the New York landscape, with Robert Moses. Moses, as the chairman of New York's Slum Clearance Committee, set his developer's eye on Lincoln Square on the Upper West Side. In 1955 the city granted permission to the committee to develop the square, and in 1956 Lincoln Center for the Performing Arts, Inc. was formed, with John D. Rockefeller III as its president.

Like the Metropolitan Museum of Art or the Natural History Museum, Lincoln Center has grown in stages. Even before the first building appeared, however, the cultural crème of New York agreed to become constituents of the planned complex: the New York Philharmonic-Symphony Society, the Juilliard School, the Metropolitan Opera Association.

Philharmonic Hall (now Avery Fisher Hall), designed by Max Abra-

Lincoln Center for the Performing Arts, Inc. 70 Lincoln Center Plaza at 65th Street Manhattan

Administration: (212) 875-5000 Tickets: (212) 721-6500

movitz, opened in 1962 and replaced Carnegie Hall as the home of the New York Philharmonic orchestra. Next, Philip Johnson's iconic Lincoln Center Fountain opened in 1964, followed by the New York State Theater in the same year, which housed the New York City Ballet. More buildings followed in quick succession: the Vivian Beaumont Theater and the Forum in 1965; the Library and Museum of the Performing Arts in 1965; the Metropolitan Opera House in 1966; Damrosch Park and the Guggenheim Band Shell in 1969; Alice Tully Hall in 1969; and the Juilliard School in 1969.

Today the center covers over sixteen acres, in a menagerie of buildings that houses some of the city's most preeminent arts organizations: the aforementioned New York Philharmonic, Juilliard School, Metropolitan Opera, and New York City Ballet, plus seven others.

SUBWAY

The New York City subway system is an underestimated marvel of modern engineering. With millions of commuters using the subway every day (about five million per weekday or 1.5 billion annually), it's easy to take for granted the dizzying breadth of its rails: 26 routes; 468 stations; 6,200 subway cars; and 660 miles of track in use. According to the Metropolitan Transit Authority, which operates the system and leases it from the City of New York, a person can travel 31 miles on the A train, from 207th Street in Manhattan to Far Rockaway in Queens, and never switch trains or actually leave New York City.

The rails—once elevated and ground level and now mostly underground, especially in Manhattan—also serve as the home of some of New York's greatest legends and mysteries: a rat population of unimaginable proportions; hidden, forgotten tunnels; and the mole people reportedly living in the anonymous tunnels and described by Jennifer Toth in her book, *The Mole People: Life in the Tunnels Beneath New York City.* It has appeared in movies, anything from 1949's *On the Town* with

The Metropolitan Transportation Authority Headquarters: (212) 878-7000

Travel information: (718) 330-1234 www.mta.info

Frank Sinatra and Gene Kelly to 1990's *Teenage Mutant Ninja Turtles,* as well as countless songs, such as "Take the A Train," by the Duke Ellington Orchestra and Ella Fitzgerald.

Every New Yorker, it seems, has a story about riding the subway. Joseph Caracciolo, in 1989, delivered a baby on a C train stalled in the Rockaways. David Hoyt, a raw-food enthusiast, became famous in a 2006 *New York Magazine* article as one of the proliferate subway flashers. There are couples who met on their daily commute, exchanging furtive glances while pretending to read the *Times,* and there are couples who loudly broke up on the subway, exiting at different stops. The subway is one of New York's most democratic media, in fact, where everyone—rich, poor, from uptown, from downtown, Manhattanites, Brooklynites, English-speakers, Spanish-speakers, natives, tourists, even the occasional celebrity—is, for a few minutes, in the exact same circumstances: hurtling through the subterranean labyrinth beneath the city in a metal pod, together until the doors open and they go their separate ways.

GROUND ZERO

The World Trade Center was a complex of seven buildings developed by the Port Authority of New York and New Jersey in the 1960s and 1970s. This set of buildings included two towers that briefly became the tallest buildings in the world until the completion of the Sears Tower in Chicago between 1973 and 1974. The northern tower, including the spire on top of its roof, reached 1,727 feet, and the pair of towers became a familiar anchor to the panorama of New York's skyline from every direction.

The events of September 11, 2001 are known worldwide. Terrorists hijacked four commercial passenger airplanes with the intent of flying them into and destroying the World Trade Center towers, the Pentagon, and reportedly the U.S. Capitol Building. They flew two airplanes into the World Trade Center's twin towers and destroyed them, killing more than 2,800 people in New York and a total of about 3,000 people over the four targets.

Everyone in New York that day

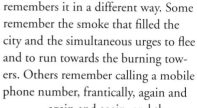

*Ground Zero
Church Street,
between Liberty
and Vesey Streets
www.wtc.com*

remembers it in a different way. Some remember the smoke that filled the city and the simultaneous urges to flee and to run towards the burning towers. Others remember calling a mobile phone number, frantically, again and again and again, and the immense relief when their father or mother or wife or husband or child finally picked up on the other end. And some people remember calling and calling and never receiving an answer.

Ground Zero is the site of the former towers, in lower Manhattan's financial district, which has become a memorial and a tourist attraction. The city is planning on building five towers in the area of the site, with the spiraling Freedom Tower as the centerpiece, as well as a new transportation hub and a memorial park. Those who peer through the fence surrounding Ground Zero can no longer see rubble and debris, but construction workers, cranes, and the beginning of something new.

THE FIRE DEPARTMENT OF NEW YORK (FDNY)

In 1648 a fire ordinance from the Dutch settlement of New Amsterdam established the first organized firefighting service. By 1658 the service consisted of bucket brigades that quelled blazes in the settlement using ladders, hooks, and leather buckets made by local shoemakers. The settlement required male citizens to serve in the brigades if they were physically fit, and the citizen firemen would run through the streets carrying ladders with buckets hanging from them, which greatly limited their response time.

In 1737 the city—now a British colony called New York—established the volunteer Fire Department of the City of New York, which continued to exist in an altered form after the Revolutionary War. In 1865 the State Legislature passed a bill that allowed a paid department called the Metropolitan Fire Department to replace the volunteer forces. In 1870 the Tweed Charter granted autonomy to New York City,

The Fire Department of New York 9 Metrotech Center, near Flatbush and Myrtle Avenues Brooklyn (718) 999-2117

abolishing all state control and, with it, the Metropolitan Fire District. In its place arose the Fire Department of the City of New York, which gave rise to the modern abbreviation FDNY, which was stenciled onto the department's equipment.

Known as New York's Bravest, the firefighters of New York have risen to daunting challenges throughout the city's history, such as the great fire of 1835 that destroyed the New York Stock Exchange or the attacks of September 11, 2001. Today the FDNY is the largest municipal fire department in the world, with 221 stations and over 340 engines and trucks. With 14,200 officers, firefighters, and emergency medical personnel, the department responds to approximately 500,000 emergency calls every year, with a response time of four to six minutes—a many-fold improvement over the seventeenth-century fire brigades that traveled to fires by foot and extinguished them using buckets and hand pumps.

THE BIG APPLE

Like the I ♥ NY slogan, the moniker "The Big Apple" became popular in the 1970s due to a promotional campaign from the New York Convention and Visitors Bureau. Unlike the I ♥ NY campaign, however, no one has traced its origin with certainty.

The common explanation for New York's nickname traces back to John Fitz Gerald, a journalist in the early twentieth century. In the 1920s he wrote about horse racing for the *New York Morning Telegraph* and referred to the city as "The Big Apple." He even titled one of his columns "Around the Big Apple," wherein he wrote on February 18, 1924: "The Big Apple. The dream of every lad that ever threw a leg over a thoroughbred and the goal of all horsemen. There's only one Big Apple. That's New York."

Supposedly Fitz Gerald had picked up the term from stable hands in New Orleans, who dreamed of eventually moving to New York, home of the most thriving racetrack scene in the country. After Fitz Gerald exposed his readers to the nickname, jazz musicians picked it up, referring to the city as the big apple of musical gigs. The Big Apple especially applied to Harlem, where a club by the same name opened in the 1930s.

In 1997 former Mayor Rudolph Giuliani even imprinted the name onto New York City geography by naming the corner of 54th Street and Broadway "Big Apple Corner"—chosen because Fitz Gerald used to live at that address. The Fitz Gerald theory is the most common explanation for the city's comparison to an oversize fruit, although another theory ascribes it to a passage in *The Wayfarer,* by Edward Martin, published in 1909. No matter where the name originated, however, "The Big Apple" is a great improvement over the city's previous nickname, "Fun City."

FLATIRON

Not many tourists—and only slightly more New Yorkers—will recognize the name of the Fuller Building. Designed by Daniel Burnham and named after George Fuller, the founder of the construction company that built it, the Fuller Building quickly received a new name from the public due to its unique triangular shape: the Flatiron Building.

The Fuller (Flatiron) Building 175 Fifth Avenue at 23rd Street Manhattan

After its completion in 1902, the building created quite a hubbub within the city, with many skeptics who believed that the first strong wind would topple the building. Mark Twain wrote in the *New York Times* in 1905: "Humor, to be comprehensible to anybody, must be built upon a foundation with which he is familiar. If he can't see the foundation the superstructure is to him merely a freak—like the Flatiron building without any visible means of support—something that ought to be arrested."

The building is rather like Clark Kent in this sense. The public saw the Flatiron as weak and susceptible, but the building included an internal steel cage for support—the first of its kind—that was invisible to the public.

Today the twenty-two-story Flatiron building houses mostly publishing firms, such as St. Martin's Press, and shops on the ground floor. It is one of the most photographed locations in New York City (notably recorded by photographers Alfred Stieglitz and Edward Steichen) and has appeared in the Spider-Man films as the home of the newspaper the *Daily Bugle.* And despite the portents of doom from New Yorkers at the beginning of the twentieth century, the building still has not blown over.

NEW YORK BOTANICAL GARDEN

First, there was the Garden of Eden. And then the royal gardens of Egypt, the Hanging Gardens of Babylon, the plant collection of Chinese Emperor Shen Nung, and the botanical garden in Athens maintained by Aristotle, the Greek philosopher.

The concept of the botanical garden dates back to the origin of humankind. Like Eden, gardens have always served as an earthly paradise: Nebuchadnezzar II, for example, supposedly built the Hanging Gardens of Babylon as a refuge for his wife, Amytis of Media. But they have also served a very practical function, especially in relatively recent history: Around the sixteenth century, universities began using gardens for the study of medicine, which was closely related to botany at the time.

In the summer of 1888, two New Yorkers visited the famous Kew Royal Botanic Gardens in England and returned with the determination to build their own botanical garden in their growing city. Nathaniel Lord Britton and his wife, Elizabeth Knight Britton,

The New York Botanical Garden 200th Street and Kazimiroff Boulevard Bronx (718) 817-8700 www.nybg.org

spearheaded the project to build the gardens in the northernmost region of the city, and received municipal funding as well as private support from well-known tycoons of the day such as Andrew Carnegie, Cornelius Vanderbilt, and John Pierpont Morgan.

The New York Botanical Garden in the Bronx has achieved many noteworthy accomplishments since its founding, such as the completion of the Haupt Conservatory in 1902, a Victorian glasshouse that became a New York City Landmark in 1973. (The garden itself is a National Historic Landmark.) Spanning 250 acres, it is a place of both research and leisure, as the charter states, "for the collection and culture of plants, flowers, shrubs and trees, [and] the advancement of botanical science and knowledge . . . and for the entertainment, recreation, and instruction of the people." It houses tropical rain forest and desert exhibits, conifers and crabapples, daffodils and daylilies. A few dozen scientists and graduate students also work on the grounds, utilizing the Mertz Library, Steere Herbarium, and extensive grounds.

ZABAR'S

Zabar's began in 1934 as a fish counter at the Daitch Market, where the store is still located today. Louis and Lillian Zabar, both Ukrainian immigrants, opened the stall to sell high-quality smoked fish at reasonable prices. Their venture proved successful, and the Zabars eventually took over the Daitch Market and named it Zabar's. Besides smoked fish, for which Zabar's is still famous, the store now sold a range of items, all hand-chosen by Louis Zabar; he reportedly even roasted his own coffee.

Zabar's
2245 Broadway
at 80th Street
Manhattan
(212) 787-2000
www.zabars.com

After Louis died in 1950, his sons Saul and Stanley took over. Eli Zabar, Louis and Lillian's youngest son, was still in secondary school at the time. He helped at the store, but after graduating from Columbia in 1967, he opened a new line of businesses including E.A.T. restaurant on Madison Avenue and Eli's Vinegar Factory on 91st Street.

Now, the third generation of Zabars is inheriting the store, which occupies a large section of the block between 80th and 81st Streets—a stretch of real estate along Broadway that Louis had acquired gradually, steadily, through years of hard work.

You can call Zabar's a deli, or you can call it a specialty foods store, a grocery store, or a kitchen appliances store. All of these titles are appropriate, but nowadays the Upper West Side bursts with delis and specialty food stores and still Zabar's maintains its originality. First of all, it is among the first and finest stores of its kind—specialty food stores have proliferated in recent years, but Louis Zabar's original concept was visionary back in the mid-twentieth century.

Second of all, the store has become stitched into the fabric of the city. Even for New Yorkers who don't shop there, it is a familiar constant in a rapidly changing city: It is a neighbor, a family tradition, a comforting story that everyone knows.

THE APOLLO THEATER

When the Apollo Theater opened in 1914, it was owned by two Jewish men, Jules Hurtig and Harry Seamon. It operated as Hurtig and Seamon's New Burlesque Theatre and allowed only white patrons. It is ironic, then, that in the 1930s the theater—now called the Apollo and under new ownership—would become a center of black culture: not only a venue that launches careers, but a keystone of Harlem culture.

In 1934 the theater allowed black people into the audience for the first time. It hosted a "colored review" that year and also began Amateur Nite Hour at the Apollo, an adaptation of Ralph Cooper's popular radio show. According to the Apollo Theater, Ella Fitzgerald was among the first amateur-night winners.

The Apollo continued to launch the careers of legends—Billie Holiday, James Brown, Diana Ross and the

The Apollo Theater 253 West 125th Street at Seventh Avenue Manhattan (212) 531-5300 www.apollo theater.org

Supremes, The Jackson 5, Patti LaBelle, Marvin Gaye, Stevie Wonder, Aretha Franklin, Mariah Carey, The Isley Brothers, and Lauryn Hill, to name a few—and entered the realm of myth in the process.

Only slightly less famous than current Apollo performers such as Margaret Cho, Bill Cosby, Eddie Izzard, or Wynton Marsalis is a well-rubbed tree stump that often sits to one side of the stage. The stump is a segment of the Tree of Hope, an elm that used to stand between Connie's Inn and the Harlem Lafayette Theater between 131st and 132nd Streets along Seventh Avenue. Black performers used to touch the tree for good luck before a show. After the city cut down the tree in 1934 when Seventh Avenue was expanded, the now-famous Apollo stump found its way to the theater, where performers continue to rub it for luck.

Open Auditions for Amateur Night
& *Showtime at the Apollo*
T.V. Exposure & $25,000 Grand Prize
December 1, 2007 8am First 200 acts seen
For more info. (212) 531-5370 or ApolloTheater.org

NEW YORK CITY MARATHON

In 1970 Gary Muhrcke paid $1 to enter the New York City Marathon. He started in Central Park on September 13, lined up against 127 other runners. Fifty-five men and no women completed the four laps of Central Park that made up the course. Gary Muhrcke finished first, with a time of 2:31:38, and won a wristwatch for the accomplishment.

Now the New York City Marathon is the largest in the world. The course winds through all five boroughs, starting at the mouth of the Verrazano-Narrows Bridge on Staten Island and ending in Manhattan's Central Park. The New York Road Runners, the organization that operates the race, now has to limit the number of entrants to 37,000—chosen in part by lottery—and the first-place prize for the men's and women's divisions is $130,000 each, plus appearance bonuses for recruited runners.

Since the first humble marathon in 1970, the event has become a career-launching race, hosting such legends as nine-time winner Grete Waitz, the collector of international marathon titles Uta Pippig, four-time winner Bill Rod-

The ING New York City Marathon
(212) 423-2249
www.nyc marathon.org

The New York Road Runners
(212) 860-4455
www.nyrr.org

gers, and countless others, including the 2007 newsmakers Martin Lel from Kenya, who won the marathon previously in 2003, and Paula Radcliffe from England, who holds ten world records.

Besides the hundreds of thousands of men and women who have run or rolled the marathon (the Road Runners added a wheelchair-or-hand-cycle division in 2000), perhaps the greatest legend of the marathon is Fred Lebow, the race's founder. He ran his inaugural marathon in 1970, finishing in forty-fifth place with a time of 4:12:09. After being diagnosed in 1990 with brain cancer, he ran the marathon one more time—to celebrate his 60th birthday—accompanied by Grete Waitz.

Fred Lebow died in 1994 of brain cancer. A statue of him now sits in Central Park, on 90th Street and the East Drive, where he looks at his watch, timing the runners who cross his path. His memorial service, held at the finish line of the race in the year of his death, attracted thousands, the largest memorial gathering in Central Park since the death of John Lennon—a testament to his legacy.

CONEY ISLAND

The name of Coney Island is as wily as the place itself. First of all, it's not an island. It's a peninsula attached to the southernmost point of Brooklyn, like a foot dipping its toes into lower New York Bay. As for the Coney half of its name, no one knows for certain its origin. One theory suggests that a late eighteenth-century Irishman named it after an island a mile from his hometown of Sligo. Another theory holds that Coney evolved from *konijn,* the Dutch word for rabbit, which once overran the island as well as other regions of Long Island.

No matter where it came from, the name Coney Island has become synonymous with all the fantasies and wonders one can imagine—from the prude to the prurient. Even in the nineteenth century, Coney Island was a place of happy seaside entertainment mixed with darker undercurrents. The Elephant Hotel stood at the center of local prostitution, while amusement parks like Sea-Lion Park, Luna Park, and Dreamland sprung up along the boardwalk.

The beach bloomed throughout the early 1900s. Nathan Handwerker opened the first Nathan's Hot Dogs

Coney Island USA
(718) 372-5159
www.coneyisland
.com

Astroland
(718) 372-0275
www.astroland
.com

in 1916 near Stillwell Avenue (in fact, Charles Feltman invented the hot dog at Coney Island in 1867) and began the now-famous hot-dog-eating contest. The Wonder Wheel, a 150-foot Ferris wheel with both stationary and swinging cars, opened in 1920, and the legendary Cyclone roller coaster opened in 1927. The amusement park Astroland USA opened in 1967 and still exists today.

Yet, development has always threatened the unique character of Coney Island. New Yorkers have fought for the area's preservation and protection as the embodiment of classical amusement and burlesque entertainment, and as the refuge of bizarre characters. Nevertheless, every year women in glittery mermaid costumes and men with tridents march in the Mermaid Parade as if it might be their last; every summer when people form a line for blocks along Surf Avenue to ride the Cyclone, they wonder if it will reopen next year. It is this potential for loss that makes Coney Island so special to New Yorkers, because it is not just a beach lined with freaks and fantasies—it is a part of us that will disappear unless we fight for it.

STATEN ISLAND FERRY

In 1817 residents of Staten Island could cross New York Bay to Manhattan for 25 cents aboard the *Nautilus,* a steam ferry commanded by Captain John De Forest. This is the same price residents paid in 1975 to make the round-trip journey, 5.2 miles in each direction, aboard fuel-powered modern ferries operated by the New York City Department of Transportation. (De Forest was, incidentally, the brother-in-law of Cornelius Vanderbilt, who bought the ferry in 1838, when it was operated by the Richmond Turnpike Company.)

In 1997 the Department of Transportation eliminated the fare altogether and the ferry is now free. The ferry makes 110 trips and transports 65,000 passengers every weekday, nineteen million annually. Its route passes by the Statue of Liberty, Ellis Island, Governors Island, and the Verrazano-Narrows Bridge, and provides some of the best views of Man-

Staten Island
Ferry
New York City
Department of
Transportation
St. George
Ferry Terminal
1 Bay Street
Staten Island
(212) NEW-YORK
or 311 within
the city
www.nyc.gov

hattan and Brooklyn.

Other than its constant and faithful shuttling between Saint George's terminal on Staten Island and Whitehall Street in lower Manhattan, the ferry has served the city on other occasions, most recently after the attacks on the World Trade Center on September 11, 2001. On the day of the attacks, the ferry transported tens of thousands from lower Manhattan to Staten Island, even amidst the blinding black smoke billowing from the collapsed towers. The following day, September 12, passenger service ceased and the fleet transported emergency personnel, military personnel, and equipment to and from lower Manhattan.

The trip between Staten Island and Manhattan now takes twenty-five minutes and remains a secret among non-commuting New Yorkers who realize that they can see the Statue of Liberty, Ellis Island, and the Manhattan skyline for free.

UNISPHERE

The Unisphere was the central symbol of the 1964–65 New York World's Fair, which was headed by Robert Moses, one of the most powerful and most controversial engineers of New York City and its surrounding suburbs.

The construction of the 1939 World's Fair transformed a swampy dump in the center of Queens into what is now Flushing Meadows–Corona Park, the second-largest park in New York City. At the center of the 1939 fair sat the Unisphere's predecessor, the Perisphere (in fact, World's Fairs have called into existence several of the world's memorable structures: the Crystal Palace in London, the Eiffel Tower in Paris, the Space Needle in Seattle).

The U.S. Steel Corporation built the Unisphere on the site of the demolished Perisphere for the 1964 fair. Designed by Gilmore Clarke, this stainless-steel model of Earth rose twelve stories high and weighed 450 tons including its pedestal—the largest representation of the globe ever attempted at the time and the largest structure made out of stainless steel. The three rings orbiting the sphere represented the first NASA

Flushing Meadows Corona Park Queens

New York City Department of Parks & Recreation (212) NEW-YORK www.nycgov parks.org

satellites to orbit the Earth, although there are multiple interpretations of their significance.

At a press conference before the launch of the fair, Robert Moses said: "[The Unisphere] had to be of the space age; it had to reflect interdependence of men on planet Earth; and it had to emphasize their achievements and aspirations."

The Unisphere fell into disrepair over the years, gathering layers of graffiti and grime. In 1989 park officials noted that "on windy days the tips of India and Vietnam lift off their mountings." The New York City Department of Parks and Recreation began a fifteen-year, $80-million restoration of the park in 1994, which included a revitalization of the Unisphere. They cleaned and reinforced the structure, relandscaped the surrounding area, and doubled the number of spray jets in the fountain where it rests.

The Unisphere rose again into a position of noble standing. It has become a predominant symbol of Queens and one of its most notable attractions.

THE NEW YORK
POLICE DEPARTMENT (NYPD)

The New York Police Department has one of the most difficult jobs in the United States. Its mission is to "enhance the quality of life in our City by working in partnership with the community and in accordance with constitutional rights to enforce the law, preserve the peace, reduce fear, and provide a safe environment for all people who live, work, or visit this City."

Enforcing the law sometimes requires the use of force. This gives rise to the dichotomy of the NYPD. On one hand, they represent the strong arm of fraternal protection—like an older sibling, willing to use any means to protect the residents of New York City. On the other hand, the misuse of their power has led to incidents of corruption and brutality.

Examples of both faces of the NYPD appear in the media. Corruption in the NYPD made headlines, for example, with the Tammany Hall political machine of the late nineteenth century or the violence against protesters in Tompkins Square Park in 1988.

The New York
Police
Department
1 Police Plaza
Manhattan
Switchboard:
(646) 610-5000
www.nyc.gov

But these headlines often obfuscate the other face of the NYPD, the face of police officers who risk their lives every day for the protection and care of New York City.

The terrorist attacks of September 11, 2001, reminded New York about the noble face of "New York's Finest." In the attack, 343 firefighters, twenty-three police officers, and thirty-seven Port Authority police officers died, according to *Newsday*. In light of the brave sacrifice of these men and women, New Yorkers remembered how heavy a burden they have placed upon the city's rescue workers and law enforcement.

Today there are approximately 38,000 uniformed officers to guard a city of 469 square miles and over eight million people. Their duties range from dangerous investigations into organized crime to maintaining order in Times Square on New Year's Eve. Like teachers, police officers do not always receive the recognition they deserve, because it is a difficult job that not just anyone could do and do well.

THE DAKOTA

The Dakota building on Manhattan's Upper West Side has appeared in newspaper headlines many times, although four incidences stick out in New York mythology.

The Dakota first made the news in 1884, when developer Edward Clarke completed the building, with a complete roster of tenants already in hand. The apartment building marked a new direction for luxury living in New York City, a divergence from private homes with servants to full-service apartments. Its French interior fully matched the grandeur of its North German Renaissance exterior, and the building—despite its then remote location—quickly filled. Since its opening, the Dakota has attracted the city's wealthiest and most prominent citizens, including celebrities Andrew Carnegie, Judy Garland, Leonard Bernstein, Lauren Bacall, Paul Simon, Gilda Radner, Carson McCullers, and Rudolf Nureyev.

The next predominant Dakota headline occurred when director Roman Polanski released his film *Rosemary's Baby* in 1968. Even though Polanski used a Hollywood soundstage for the

The Dakota
1 West 72nd
Street at Central
Park West
Manhattan

Strawberry Fields
New York City
Department
of Parks &
Recreation
(212) NEW-YORK
www.nycgov
parks.org

interior scenes, and despite his premise of Satan worshipers occupying the Dakota, the film further cemented the building as one of the most prominent addresses in New York City. Its reputation grew even more when it became a National Historic Landmark on December 8, 1976—the third memorable appearance of the building in the newspapers.

Yet it is the fourth news appearance of the Dakota that makes it more than a building. On December 8, 1980, a taxicab pulled up to the building's front gate and let out two of its residents, John Lennon and Yoko Ono. As they entered the building, Mark David Chapman fired five bullets at Lennon, four of which met their target.

John Lennon died that night, an event that upset the nation on the same scale as the assassination of John F. Kennedy or Martin Luther King Jr. Across Central Park West from the Dakota, at 72nd Street, there is now a memorial to John Lennon—an area of the park called Strawberry Fields, after his song "Strawberry Fields Forever."

HOT DOGS

There are multiple stories for the origin of hot dogs, and one story probably bears as much truth as the others, but New Yorkers maintain that hot dogs began in Brooklyn, when Charles Feltman started selling sausages in rolls in 1867. In 1912 Feltman hired a Polish immigrant named Nathan Handwerker to work in his Coney Island restaurant.

Handwerker's name would eventually become a New York institution and synonymous with hot dogs nationwide. In 1916 he opened Nathan's Famous hot dog stand on Coney Island. That same year, according to the Nathan's Famous corporation, four of his customers held an impromptu hot-dog-eating contest on July 4, Independence Day. The four customers, all immigrants, decided that whoever could eat the most hot dogs was the most American among them. James Mullen from Ireland won by eating thirteen hot dogs in twelve minutes.

Nathan's Famous
1310 Surf Avenue
at Stillwell
Avenue
Brooklyn
(718) 946-2202
www.nathans
famous.com

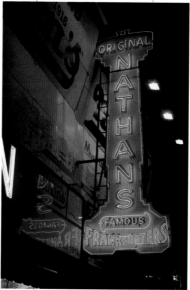

The Nathan's Famous hot-dog-eating contest has occurred every year on Independence Day since 1916 at Nathan's flagship store at the corner of Surf and Stillwell Avenues. In 2007 Joey Chestnut defeated the six-time champion Takeru Kobayashi by eating sixty-six hot dogs in twelve minutes, setting a world record in the process.

Nathan's hot dogs now define the product itself, just as Band-Aid stands for adhesive bandages or Kleenex stands for tissues. They have attracted the attention of President Franklin Roosevelt, who served them to the king and queen of England, Barbra Streisand, who served them at a private party, and Nelson Rockefeller, who visited the stand while campaigning for reelection as governor and said, "No man can hope to get elected in New York State without being photographed eating hot dogs at Nathan's Famous."

WALL STREET

Wall Street is more than a street in lower Manhattan. It has become a persona, an embodiment of the might and mystery of finance, not just in New York, but in the United States. The Wall Street of today began in 1792, when a group of twenty-four merchants formed a private trading group that would eventually become the New York Stock Exchange. The tip of New York had already served as a center of commerce, but the formation of the stock exchange marked a new direction for finance in the city.

The power of the stock exchange grew—to be joined in 1842 by the American Stock Exchange, in 1870 by the New York Cotton Exchange, and years later by the National Association of Securities Dealers Automated Quotations in 1971. Around the turn of the twentieth century, the trading of stocks and commodities had launched the fortunes of cunning investors like banking tycoon J. P. Morgan.

An institution that seemingly has the power to raise the country into opulent prosperity also has the ability

Wall Street (the Financial District) Bounded by the West Side Highway, Vesey Street, the East River, and State Street
Manhattan

to throw it into chaos. In 1929 the economic bubble of long-term speculation in the market burst and caused the stock market to crash, throwing the country into the Great Depression—a downturn that affected the entire country, not just Wall Street brokers.

Today, even though national finance has diffused somewhat into other parts of New York or to other cities, Wall Street—the financial district named after its most famous artery—still observes the flow of billions of dollars every day. Wall Street has transformed in the digital age—it is less focused on the crazed trading floors of yesteryear and more on the crazed computer terminals of financial firms. It also contains several landmarks of city history: Trinity Church at the intersection of Broadway and Wall Street, the American Stock Exchange at 86 Trinity Place, Federal Hall at 26 Wall Street (the first Capitol of the United States), the Woolworth building at 233 Broadway, Arturo Di Modica's charging-bull sculpture on Bowling Green, and Ground Zero, the former site of the World Trade Center.

AMERICAN MUSEUM OF NATURAL HISTORY

In the mid-nineteenth century, the emergence of naturalists such as Charles Darwin and Gregor Mendel inspired institutions nationwide to record evolutionary and geological history. Harvard University, for example, founded the Museum of Contemporary Zoology in 1859, under the direction of zoologist Louis Agassiz.

Albert Bickmor, who studied under Agassiz at Harvard and once worked at the Museum of Contemporary Zoology, lobbied with the patrician class of New York City for the construction of its own museum dedicated to zoological sciences. He garnered the support of J. P. Morgan, William Dodge, Theodore Roosevelt Sr., and fifteen other New York philanthropists, and in 1869 Governor John Hoffman passed the legislation to create the American Museum of Natural History.

The complex of buildings that comprise the museum have arisen in many stages and just as many architectural styles. The first building, a neo-Gothic structure completed in 1877,

American Museum of Natural History Central Park West and 79th Street Manhattan (212) 769-5100 www.amnh.org

came from architects Jacob Mould and Calvert Vaux (who co-designed Central Park with Frederick Law Olmsted). Subsequent buildings followed, in Romanesque, beaux arts, and American Renaissance styles.

The museum now occupies twenty-five buildings in Manhattan Square, between 77th and 81st Streets off of Central Park West. It boasts over thirty-two million specimens, although the museum displays only a fraction of them to the public. The museum stores the remaining items in its collection in its labyrinthine storage and research facilities.

Some of the most popular attractions at the museum include the dinosaur fossils on the fourth floor (as well as the rearing *Barosaurus* in the main entrance hall), the life-size 94-foot-long blue whale in the Hall of Ocean Life, the halls of minerals and gems, the annual Butterfly Conservatory, and the Rose Center and Planetarium, completed in 2000 on the site of the original Hayden Planetarium.

NEW YORK CITY SKYLINE

A stadium is a stadium and a statue is a statue, but the Manhattan skyline is amorphous and always changing—a barometer of urban development. The other boroughs have their own skylines, of course—the water towers of Brooklyn or the varied topography of the Bronx—but it is the silhouette of Manhattan that distinguishes New York City from other metropolitan landscapes.

Like Hong Kong, San Francisco, or Seattle, Manhattan's unique waterbound geography has, in part, caused its vertical ascension. Approaching the southern tip of Manhattan from Staten Island, the city appears as a cluster of skyscrapers huddled together on an island no wider than 2 miles. From New Jersey or Brooklyn, however, the city stretches methodically across the horizon, with its sundry towers reaching up and calling to the stars. The distinctive tiered shape of the Chrysler Building, the three-color glow of the Empire State Building, the

neon blaze of Times Square, the disciplined vertical growth of the financial district, the modest height of the East and West Villages—if you read them like Braille, they tell a story. The story varies whether you read the city from left to right or right to left. It also varies from person to person—no one will scan the peaks and valleys of Manhattan and interpret them the same way.

It is impossible to drive over the Brooklyn Bridge, with the city laid out bare, without thinking about the stories that build a city: the grand and fantastic stories of Vanderbilts and Rockefellers, the equally important stories of the working and immigrant classes, the stories of dreams both accomplished and deferred. But the skyline is the one icon in this book that disappears when you approach it. Once you drive over the bridge, you dive into the city and it surrounds you. You become a part of it, this city of parts and dreams.